Alan Turing: Enigma

The Incredible True Story of the Man Who Cracked The Code

Anna Revell

Introduction

If you have ever used a computer, you owe that joy to Alan Turing. Turing is known by many as the Father of the Modern Computer for his conception of the theoretical stored-memory machine (known as the Turing Machine) and for the subsequent implementation of this idea in the creation of some of the world's first working computers, the Automatic Computing Engine, and the Manchester Mark 1.

Essentially, Turing not only conceived of the possible existence of a computer that could perform more than one task, he was also instrumental in helping several computer labs actually bring his ideas to life. He saw his concepts go from mere theory to actual reality in his lifetime. Everything he theorized was then built on by new generations of computer scientists, and eventually led to the technological wonderland in which we live, and often take for granted, today.

Impressive as they are, though, Turing's contributions to computer science are not necessarily his most famous or influential projects. Alan Turing was one of the most significant figures in the Allied victory of World War Two, thanks to his ingenious code breaking skills and the invention of the British Bombe at Bletchley Park. In his later life, Turing even dabbled in artificial intelligence, and biology, creating concepts that are still being investigated today.

Until recently, Alan Turing had often been overlooked as an important figure in history. Thanks to in-depth biographies like Andrew Hodges' *Alan Turing: The Enigma*, and film depictions of Turing's life, like *The Imitation Game*, based on Hodges' book, Alan Turing is quickly becoming a household name, as people begin to recognize that his contributions to various fields were so influential they actually changed the course of human history.

Early Life

Alan Mathison Turing was born on June 23rd, 1912 at Warrington Lodge, a nursing home in Paddington, England. The Turings, Ethel and Julius, were temporarily back in England at the time, while Julius took leave from his work in the Indian Civil Service in British India. Ethel wanted her children, Alan and his brother John, to be born and grow up, in England.

Alan was an absent-minded, stubborn, and precocious child. He paid little attention to what other other people around him wanted. He often delayed his mother or nanny for long periods of time while they were out running errands just so he could carefully inspect small things like lamppost serial numbers. As careless as he could be, he was also detail-oriented, curious, meticulous, and, when something grabbed his attention, singularly-focused.

His nanny later remarked on "his integrity and his intelligence for a child so young" after Alan got extremely upset when he noticed she had let him win at a game. It was remarkable that a child so young even noticed he was being fooled, and even more remarkable that he respected the game play so much.

Alan's independent nature didn't lend itself to traditional schooling. He wanted to study what he was interested in, when he wanted to study it, not what the school told him to learn, when they told him to learn it.

At age 10 Alan was sent to Hazelhurst, the preparatory school his brother John was attending at the time. John was a popular boy, and a good student. He even became head boy at the time Alan joined him at the school.

In 1922 Alan got his hands on a book that would change his life. *Natural Wonders Every Child Should Know* was an American science text for children. The book basically opened Alan's eyes to the existence of science as a study, and a legitimate pursuit. It also introduced the idea that God had less to do with natural phenomena than Alan had been taught his whole life. Alan devoured this book and took it with him wherever he went.

Unfortunately for Alan, science was not a focus in British schools at the time. He was pushed to study language, including Latin, and classics. His parents allegedly weren't displeased with his interest in science. They encouraged his passion, buying him a chemistry set for Christmas in 1924, and attempting to answer what questions they could.

Alan's mother has said that she recognized and encouraged his genius from the beginning. His brother, however, completely refutes this claim. He said, "The truth of the matter, as I now view it in retrospect, is that neither of Alan's parents or his brother had the faintest idea that this tiresome, eccentric and obstinate small boy was a budding genius". He claimed their mother was constantly "trying to press him into a conventional mould." After his death, Alan's journals would reveal that he severely disliked his mother, possibly because she was not as nurturing of his talents as she claimed to be.

Whether or not the Turings encouraged Alan's scientific genius is up for debate. What is certain is that they wanted Alan to get into a good public school. This would require Alan to pass the Common Entrance Exam, a test that focused on languages and classics rather than science or math.

Alan continued his interest in science, but also studied for the entrance exam. He took it once in 1925 and did fairly well; and again in 1926 after which he was accepted into Sherbrooke School in Dorset.

On his first day of Sherbrooke there was a general strike that halted trains and busses. With no way of getting to his new school, Alan opted to cycle the 60 miles from his home town to Dorset. This incredible feat foreshadowed Alan's impressive athletic ability, and was even written about in the paper. Later, when he worked at Bletchley Park, Alan would find a penchant for long distance running. He was often said to run to meetings in London that were over 40 miles from Bletchley Park, rather than take the train. He won many races in his athletic club, and was said to be a near-Olympic level marathoner.

Alan's odd personality made him fairly un-popular with his classmates. As he was still an unfocused, stubborn student, he didn't have any fans on the staff at Sherbrooke, either. His housemaster called him "undeni-ably...not a 'normal boy'".

Alan continued his interest in science and mathematics to the detriment of his other subjects. He was also uninterested in the other, more social aspects of the school in which the boys were pushed to participate. Sherbrooke was focused on moulding well-rounded citizens who were not only top students, but were social, athletic, and generally well-trained.

Nowell Smith, Sherbrooke's headmaster, wrote to the Turings and told them that Alan's singular focus on science did not fit with the Sherbrooke philosophy. He wrote, "If he is to stay at a Public School, he must aim to be educated. If he is to be solely a Scientific Specialist, he is wasting his time at a Public School."

Though he began to take more of an interest in subjects other than science, and began to do better, Alan was still held back in fifth form. He was, however, allowed to take sixth form mathematics, as that was obviously his strong suit.

In 1927 Alan began looking closely at Einstein's work questioning Galilei-Newtonian axioms. He actually managed to continue Einstein's work, and properly explain the scientist's viewpoints on the axioms that his written work never made completely clear.

It was around this time that Alan met Christopher Morcom, a fellow science enthusiast, and the man generally believed to be Alan's first love. The two studied science and mathematics together, and worked on problems in their spare time.

Christopher was more of the exemplary Sherbrooke student; social, well-rounded, and a good student in all his subjects. His interest in Christopher inspired Alan to try a little harder at the subjects that didn't interest him as much as science. Soon he was allowed to properly join the sixth form, and was delighted to have all his classes with Christopher.

Since childhood Christopher had been struggling with complications from bovine tuberculosis that he had contracted from drinking infected cow's milk. His condition had been worsening during his time at Sherbrooke. Christopher Morcom died in February of 1930. Alan was devastated by the loss of his friend, and decided to throw himself further into his studies, as he believed that is what Christopher would have wanted from him.

In a letter to Christopher's mother Alan wrote, "I am sure I could not have found anywhere another companion so brilliant and yet so charming and unconceited. I regarded my interest in my work, and in such things as astronomy (to which he introduced me) as something to be shared with him and I think he felt a little the same about me ... I know I must put as much energy if not as much interest into my work as if he were alive, because that is what he would like me to do."

It may have been partly Christopher's death that set Alan on the path that would define his entire career. Not only did Alan throw himself into his studies as a tribute to Christopher, which led to many academic opportunities, he also began thinking about what makes up a human.

Alan was a firm atheist, but, due to his friend's death, he began grappling with the concept of the spirit, and its connection with the mind and body. He became almost fascinated with his own grief, wondering how Christopher still had such a presence in his life, even though he had died. How could a man's spirit have such a pull on him when the man had ceased to exist? What is the spirit if it is not something that is connected to the physical body, and may continue to linger in one's mind after the death of the body?

Alan wrote again to Christopher's mother on the topic of the spirit saying, "Then as regards the actual connection between spirit and body I consider that the body by reason of being a living body can 'attract' and hold on to a 'spirit' whilst the body is alive and awake and the two are firmly connected. When the body is asleep I cannot guess what happens but when the body dies the 'mechanism' of the body, holding the spirit, is gone and the spirit finds a new body sooner or later perhaps immediately."

It is particularly interesting that Alan essentially called the body a "mechanism" that holds onto the spirit. Many of Alan's future projects would involve him attempting to explain or create a mechanical brain; a thinking entity that existed outside a human body. It was almost as if Alan was trying to build his concept of a spirit.

The mechanical brain idea informed his most seminal work; the concept of the Turing Machine, the implementation of that concept in the form of a stored-memory computer, and the idea of a Turing Test for artificial intelligence. Had Alan not suffered such a loss, and not ruminated on the concept of the spirit, his career may have taken a different path altogether.

Further Study

Alan kept his personal promise to the late Christopher Morcom. He studied hard and was admitted to King's College at Cambridge University, where he studied Mathematics. Finally able to study what he wanted, Alan did exceptionally well. He was elected fellow of King's College in 1935 for his dissertation that proved the central limit theorem.

Alan also felt more personally free at Cambridge. It was a more liberal and accepting environment, and Alan was able to freely have relationships with other men without fearing judgement or persecution.

Turing's most notable work at Cambridge was in his paper *On Computable Numbers, with an Application to the Entscheidungsproblem.*

In this 1939 paper, Alan developed the idea of a stored program computer. He called it a universal computing machine, but it is now more well known as a Turing Machine. It was a theoretical machine that consisted of a scanner, and a line of unlimited tape. The tape would be divided into squares that were either blank, or had one symbol on them (usually a 1 or a 0).

The scanner would look at each square individually, read the instruction programmed on the square, and perform an operation based on the four functions it would be programmed to perform. Any given square on the tape could tell the machine to either move left one square, move right one square, print a symbol on the square, or change it's state, meaning move on to the next set of instructions.

The example Turing gave in his paper can be summed up in the following table:

State	Scanned Square	Operations	Next State
a	blank	P[0], R	b
b	blank	R	c
c	blank	P[1], R	d
d	blank	R	a

In this scenario the machine would start with state 'a'; if the square it scanned was blank it would print a 0 on it, then move right one square and move onto the instructions in state 'b'; if the next square was blank, it would simply move right and move on to state 'c'; if that square was blank it would print a 1 on it, and move right again, to state 'd'; if that square was blank it would move right and loop back around to the instructions in state 'a', where it would start again.

His paper had been an answer to David Hilbert's *Entscheidungsproblem*. American mathematician Alonzo Church had also been working on the same problem at Princeton University. Church came up with a completely different, though equally valid answer. He was so impressed with Turing's work that he invited him to Princeton to work under him as a doctoral student so they may further study the problem. In September 1936, Alan moved to America to study under Church. Their work on computable functions is known as the Church-Turing thesis.

In June 1938 Alan Turing received his PhD from Princeton University with his dissertation *Systems of Logic Based on Ordinals.* In this paper Turing introduced the idea of ordinal logic.

He returned to England in 1938 and almost immediately began working for the Government Code and Cypher School. Britain declared war against the Axis powers on September 3rd, 1939. On September 4th, Alan reported to Bletchley Park to begin working on cracking the Enigma code.

The Enigma

Perhaps Alan Turing's most famous work had to do with breaking the German wartime code, known as the Enigma.

The Enigma machine was initially created by Arthur Scherbius after World War One in order to protect business secrets that were being sent across wires through Morse Code. The Enigma is a typewriter-like machine with two keypads, each housing all 26 letters. When the user presses a letter key on the bottom keypad, it generates an electric current which gets scrambled by the machine through a system of crossed wires. The machine then lights up a different letter on the top keypad. The newly generated letter then stands in for the actual letter in the code.

Unlike other letter substitution codes, though, Enigma would encode one single letter as a different letter every time that letter was pressed. There was not a simple substitution where every A in the code became a B, and every B became a C, etc. An A might become encoded as an L the first time you pressed it, and come out as a Z the next.

This feature made it harder to begin cracking the code, as cryptographers would often begin with a double letter (like the two Ls in "Hello") and work backwards from there, knowing that certain double letters are more common in certain languages than others. You would also be unable to find out what one letter stood for, and substitute that letter for every encoded letter. You couldn't know that every time an A showed up in the code it was actually a Y, as the Enigma machine would encode every A as a different letter.

The Enigma code was made even more difficult to crack because of the machine's many
parts, and the number of variations possible
for each part during the assembly of the machine. Initially each Enigma machine had
three rotors with the entire alphabet on each
of them. These could be placed into the machine in any order, with any one of the letters
as the starting point. Each of the rotors had a
ring attached to it which could be moved to
one of four different positions. The machine
also had a patch panel of letters on the front
of it. Each one of these letters would be connected via cable to another letter, and would
manipulate the path of the electrical current
flowing through the machine.

There were thousands of potential combinations. It was the perfect machine for sending
wartime messages, and it was soon co-opted

by the Nazis to communicate in the various arenas of battle.

Even with such astronomical odds, the Germans still didn't want to risk anyone cracking their code. The way each Enigma machine was assembled changed at midnight. Of course this was before automation, so the configuration for each day was found in a code book or chart that accompanied the machine, and done by hand. The chart explained in what position the rings on the rotors should be, at which letter each rotor was to begin, the order in which the rotors were to be placed in the machine, and the letter pairings for the front patch panel.

As if all that security wasn't enough, the Germans also encoded a separate Enigma start position for each individual message. It was a three letter code that corresponded to the rotor settings, that was then, itself, encrypted with the daily Enigma setting. In a cryptographic error, the new three letter position was encoded twice. The operator would receive a correspondence that looked like 6 random letters, and decipher it into two sets of the same three letters. He would then set the machine up accordingly, and finally be able to decode the actual message the other operator was attempting to send.

Using intelligence gathered from both commercial Enigma machine research and from German informants, Polish mathematician Marian Rejewski worked out that, due to the three letter code being encrypted twice, there was necessarily a relationship in the wiring of the Enigma machine between the first and fourth letters, the second and fifth, and the third and sixth.

Cryptanalyst Henryk Zygalski figured out that in about 1 out of 8 messages, one of the plaintext letters encrypted to the same letter twice. For example, the first and fourth letters would be encrypted from the same letter into the same, albeit different, letter. Maybe an ABCABC would turn into a TVDTNS. The As both became Ts. These sets were called females. From this occasional relationship between letters, Zygalski created a method to narrow down possible Enigma settings.

Though Zyglaski's method was effective, it was also done by hand which made it slow and inefficient. Rejewski created a machine that automated the process. He named it the *bomba kryptologiczna*, or the cryptologic bomb. It was a device that deduced the wiring of the Enigma machine. Each bomba represented six Enigma machines, and did the work of 100 people attempting to break the code by hand.

There are several stories as to why the machine was dubbed *bomba*. Oddly, one story says it was named after the ice-cream treat of the same name, though that doesn't make much sense as the two have absolutely nothing to do with one another.

A more likely story was told in a U.S Army report in 1945. It stated, "A machine called the "bombe" is used to expedite the solution. The first machine was built by the Poles and was a hand operated multiple enigma machine. When a possible solution was reached a part would fall off the machine onto the floor with a loud noise. Hence the name 'bombe'". It was both loud and used to speed up a process, much like a bomb.

Rejewski, though, simply claims it was called bombe "for lack of a better idea".

The Germans eventually figured out their code was being cracked and, in 1939, made two major changes to avoid the security hacks. They added two more possible rotors (IV, and V) to the army and airforce Enigma machines. This changed the possible number of rotor configurations from 6 to 60, and brought the possible combinations of the machine up to a whopping 158,962,555,217,826,360,000. For the all-important naval Enigma, the Germans added five more rotors, bringing the possible configuration of rotors up to 336, with the possible combinations of parts coming to over 180,000,000,000,000,000,000.

The Germans also stopped repeating the three letter starter code at the beginning of messages. These changes significantly affected the bomba's ability to break the En-

igma code, as the Germans had now removed the clues the machine used to deduce
the Enigma setup. The Poles then decided to
share their equipment and knowledge with
the British and French so that their allies may
continue their work, and the Germans could
be defeated.

The final blow to the Polish attempts at
cracking Enigma came in 1939 when Germany invaded Poland. The cryptanalysis office opted to destroy their research, lest the
Germans get their hands on a bomba, realize
their code had been compromised, and completely change their communications tactics.

Bletchley Park

Meanwhile, at Bletchley Park in England, Alan Turing and his team were working on their own ways to crack the Enigma code.

Bletchley Park was an English code breaking camp around 50 miles from London. It was first dubbed Bletchley Park in 1877 when Samuel Lipscomb Seckham bought the site and the mansion that sat upon the grounds. In May 1938, Hugh Sinclair, the head of MI6, bought the site with his own money after the government branch claimed they did not have the budget to buy the property.

Sinclair liked the spot for the Government Codes and Ciphers School for several reasons. It was across the street from a multi-line train station that would connect many important cities; it was far enough outside of

London to avoid being damaged in any air raid that might take place in the event of a war; it was also more or less equidistant between Cambridge and Oxford Universities, two prestigious schools from which code breakers would be recruited.

MI6 initially operated out of the ground's mansion from when they moved in on August 15th 1939. In late 1939, though, prefabricated huts began to be erected, and the boarding school near Bletchley Park, Elmers School, was acquired and used as part of the operation.

Bletchley Park was known to have been populated with the brightest minds England could muster. Of course mathematicians, statisticians, and scientists were brought aboard, but MI6 did not stop with these traditional fields. They recruited bridge experts, linguists, chess champions, historians, and many others with specific and rare bases of knowledge.

The organization even had *The Daily Telegraph* set up a cryptic crossword competition to scout for potential employees. They asked whether anyone could finish the cryptic crossword in under 12 minutes. These people were then invited to the Telegraph office to sit another crossword test. This time they were told to complete the puzzle in under six minutes. The winners of the competition were discreetly approached and asked if they would like to be involved in "a particular type of work as a contribution to the war effort".

Everyone who worked at Bletchley Park had to sign the Official Secrets Act 1938, but the secrecy did not stop there. Employees were discouraged from even speaking to each other about their individual projects.

They were told, "Do not talk at meals. Do not talk in the transport. Do not talk travelling. Do not talk in the billet. Do not talk by your own fireside. Be careful even in your Hut."

In September 1934, four influential men were recruited to work at Bletchley Park by Commander Alastair Denniston. Aside from Alan Turing, MI6 also brought on Gordon Welchman, Stuart Milner-Barry, and Hugh Alexander. They were some of the earliest recruits for the code breaking operations at Bletchley Park, and became known as The Wicked Uncles.

Gordon Welchman became the head of Hut 6, which worked cracking the German air force and army Enigma code. Irene Young, a worker in the Decoding Room of Hut 6 said, "operators were constantly having nervous breakdowns on account of the pace of the work and the appalling noise." Indeed, codebreakers at Bletchley Park worked around the clock to try and get any lead on a potential solution.

Welchman, unable to fully decipher any Enigma message, set his sights on something else. He began simple traffic analysis of the messages the team was intercepting. Welchman paid close attention to callsigns of encrypted German messages, and to where these messages were coming from, and going to. Eventually this led to Welchman deducing the callsign for a large majority of German bases, ships, outposts, and, notably, weather stations. The team at Bletchley Park began to piece together a map of the entire communications system used by the Germans.

Turing was working as the head of Hut 8, attempting to crack the naval Enigma. He knew that certain greetings, and indicators were used daily by German officers. For example, he knew that each morning a German U-boat would send out a weather report at the same time, using not only the German word for weather report (Wetterbericht), but the same order of information: wind speed, atmospheric pressure, temperature.

U-boats also often sent the message "Keine besonderen Ereignisse", or "no special occurrences." Using this information Turing was able to create what became known as cribs, basically the team's best guesses for what the Enigma layout for the day might be.

Laying an intercepted message overtop something like the German "Wetterbericht", which he knew would be going out at a certain time in the morning, Alan Turing was able to make a guess as to how the Enigma was set up for that day. Turing also noted one major flaw in the Enigma machine; it could not encrypt a letter as itself. No As became As in the encrypted code. This narrowed down thousands of possibilities for Enigma configuration. If you laid out a message and the W in "Wetterbericht" matched with another W in the encrypted code, you could be certain that was not the configuration of the Enigma machine. This was called crib dragging.

Using his knowledge of the Polish bomba, and the principles of elimination he deduced himself, known as Banburismus, Alan created the British Bombe. Like the Polish machine, the Bombe was a code breaking machine that basically ran through all the possible Enigma settings until it produced a readable, understandable plaintext, free from errors. When it had finished its job, the team would then have the Enigma configuration for the day and be able to decipher the rest of the messages that would be intercepted that day. The first British Bombe was installed in Hut 1 at Bletchley Park on March 18th, 1940.

The Bombe wasn't a magical code breaking machine. The Enigma code still had billions of possibilities for its configuration. The Bletchley team still needed cribs to kickstart the deciphering process.

As one such crib, Bletchley Park code breakers used what were known as kisses. A kiss was an identical message that was sent in two different codes, one of which had already been broken. It was called as kiss as the codebreakers designated one with a 'xx', the traditional short form for kisses in written correspondence sent to a loved one.

The German navy often used both the Enigma, and a dockyard cipher, a hand cipher which was much easier to break. Germans would send the same message out in both codes and, as Bletchley Park had most likely already broken the dockyard cipher, they could compare the two identical messages, and figure out the Enigma for the day.

Bletchley Park also acquired cribs through 'gardening'. This referred to the process of coaxing certain known words out of the Germans. The British would plant mines in certain places knowing that the Germans would send out warning messages with the locations of the mines, what area or harbor was nearby, and, probably the word 'mine'.

Again, the U-boats would send out these messages in both Enigma, and the simpler dockyard cipher. Being able to cross reference the same message in both the easier, broken cipher, and the more difficult Enigma, gave Bletchley Park valuable intel into what the Enigma setting was for the day.

Once the codebreakers collected these cribs they could then pass their best guesses through the Bombe, and the machine would run through the possibilities that remained.

At first the Bombe runs could take days. When Gordon Welchman modified Turing's initial bombe design with a diagonal board the machine was then able to cross check hundreds of possible solutions at the same time. This cut down the time it took to find the solution to the Enigma code from days to mere hours. After Welchman's modification, the codebreakers would generally have the Enigma solution for the day by the early morning, after starting at midnight when the new Enigma configurations were meant to be set.

Occasionally German officers didn't bother changing their Enigma settings from the previous day, giving Bletchley Park a huge advantage.

Turing was also able to develop the Eins Catalogue as a crib system. Bletchley Park knew, thanks to information gleaned from an interrogation of a German prisoner of war, that numbers in an Enigma cipher were always coded in complete, spelled out letters, not in abbreviations or substitutions. Turing took this information and, using backlogged broken codes, discovered that 'eins', the German word for 'one' was used in almost every message the Germans sent. It was by far the most used four letter word in their messages.

Once the rotor setting for the day had been determined there were still over 17,000 possible configurations for the word 'eins'. Alan catalogued each one of these possibilities in alphabetical order so that, if a certain string of four letters came up in a message, the codebreakers would have a possible shortcut for figuring out the rest of the code. They would pull the Enigma machine configuration from the catalogue once a possible 'eins' was found, test that configuration, and, if it produced coherent German they had cracked the code for the day.

British intelligence could not let on that they had broken the code, or that they were even attempting to do so. If the Germans realized the Allied had figured out the Enigma code they would change their communications systems, and Britain would be left in the dark with no possible way to glean new and necessary intelligence.

The Allies, therefore, had to decide which pieces of information they received were essential to winning the war, and which could be overlooked in the name of keeping their knowledge secret. Some German attacks were allowed to go on, even though the British knew they were imminent. They also sent dummy ships out to certain locations so the Germans could see the enemy vessel, and assume anything the Allies turned out to know about German locations or plans came from the ship they had seen days prior.

Unfortunately this strategy did lead to damaged ships, fewer supplies, and, most tragically, lost lives. However, many more lives were ultimately saved by letting the Germans believe their code was, indeed, unbreakable.

Since the beginning of the war German U-boats in the North Atlantic had sunk over 700 Allied ships, destroying hundreds of tonnes of supplies, and taking several lives.

Winston Churchill, the wartime British Prime Minister was quoted as saying, "...the only thing that ever really frightened me during the war was the U-boat peril." If supplies could not be moved across the Atlantic then Britain may have just been essentially starved into submission. The North Atlantic was also important for bringing troops to Europe for D-Day operations.

The loss of the naval corridor would have been disastrous for the Allies. This tension was referred to as The Battle of the Atlantic. In cracking the Enigma, the code breakers salvaged supply lines, and saved valuable supplies, ships, and lives.

In late October, 1941, The Wicked Uncles (Turing, Welchman, Alexander, and Milner-Barry) co-signed a letter addressed to Churchill explaining what their operation had done toward winning The Battle of the Atlantic, and their need for more resources to continue their work.

The letter read, "Some weeks ago you paid us the honour of a visit, and we believe that you regard our work as important. You will have seen that, thanks largely to the energy and foresight of Commander Travis, we have been well supplied with the 'bombes' for the breaking of the German Enigma codes. We think, however, that you ought to know that this work is being held up, and in some cases is not being done at all, principally because we cannot get sufficient staff to deal with it. Our reason for writing to you direct is that for months we have done everything that we possibly can through the normal channels, and that we despair of any early improvement without your intervention."

Churchill, so impressed with Bletchley Park's successes, and equally worried about losing the Atlantic supply lines immediately moved on the request. He wrote to General Ismay saying, "ACTION THIS DAY. Make sure they have all they want on extreme priority and report to me that this has been done."

By mid-November Bletchley Park had all the resources they needed to continue their essential work, though apparently the codebreakers were unaware of the Prime Minister's strong support. Milner-Barry later recalled, "All that we did notice was that almost from that day the rough ways began miraculously to be made smooth."

Alan had a brief engagement in 1941 to Joan Clarke, a fellow Hut 8 codebreaker. Clarke was mentee of Gordon Welchman at Cambridge University. He recruited her in 1940 to work at Bletchley Park. Their engagement only lasted a few months. Alan had admitted to Joan that he was gay. Joan said she was "unfazed" by the revelation and wanted to marry him anyway. Both recognized marriage as more of a social duty than an actual partnership based on romantic love. It was not necessarily commonplace at the time to marry for love, and it was quite unusual to remain single, so the arrangement worked for both parties.

Alan ultimately decided he did not want to go through with the marriage, wanting to give Joan the opportunity to be in a legitimate relationship. They dissolved their relationship, but remained close friends for the rest of Alan's life. In 1952 Joan married a colleague at her post-war job at the Government Communications Headquarters.

In February of 1942 the Nazis introduced a fourth rotor to their Enigma machine, This new configuration was codenamed Triton in Germany, and Shark in England. The extra rotor made it much more difficult to crack the code. Casualties in the North Atlantic again began to rise and Bletchley Park had to scramble to attempt to break the code of what appeared to be an entirely new machine.

Turing was sure there was to be some relationship between the old three rotor machines, and these new four rotor ones, as not all the Enigma machines across all German communication lines had been converted, yet the Germans continued to communicate with one another.

Eventually it was discovered that the fourth rotor was not a removable one, like the others, but a stationary one with only 26 possible settings. Had it been a new removable rotor, the naval Enigma rotor configurations would have increased from 336 to 3,024. It was certainly not as disastrous a change as it could have been, but still made the problem of the Enigma 26 times more difficult, and

would, thus, require 26 Bombes for every
one currently in operation.

The codebreakers did occasionally get some
insight into this new rotor. The fourth rotor
was usually set to a neutral position on U-
boats. In December 1941 Bletchley Park intercepted a message that was unintelligible,
followed by the same message in the proper
code. Bletchley Park was able to deduce that
the first message had come from the U-boat
operator accidentally knocking the fourth rotor out of the neutral position, and encoding
the incoherent message on a setting that did
not make sense.

The subsequent message allowed the
codebreakers to figure out the wiring of the
fourth rotor. This was useful information,
but did not mean the team could automatic-
ally increase their cracking speed back to

where it was before the fourth rotor was introduced. Bombe runs still sometimes took days instead of hours.

MI6 did not only rely on broken Enigma code for their intelligence. Much of the codebreaking done at Bletchley Park also used the code books and lists retrieved from sunken U-boats. Unfortunately it was not until 9 months after the switch from the three rotor machine to the four rotor machine that Britain was able to get the new books. It was clear that Bletchley Park clearly needed help with intelligence gathering.

They had been keeping their methods top secret and, even with America's entrance into the war in December of 1941, still refused to share their code breaking methods with their allies. However, with the new four rotor machine slowing down their abilities, and losses in the Atlantic increasing daily, Bletchley Park decided to show the Americans how to build their own Bombe. Alan was sent to America in November-December 1942 to aid the National Cash Register Corporation in creating a functional and secure Bombe.

Alan seemed amused at what the Americans assumed codebreaking at Bletchley Park was like. He said, "The American Bombe programme was to produce 336 Bombes, one for each wheel order. I used to smile inwardly at the conception of Bombe hut routine implied by this programme, but thought that no particular purpose would be served by pointing out that we would not really use them in that way."

Turing explained to the Americans that, using his elimination methods, they would not need 336 machines, only 96. By just a year later America had 120 Bombes. They became fast, efficient code breakers, and aided Britain greatly in cracking the German naval Enigma for the remainder of the war.

Alan returned to Bletchley Park in March 1943 as a general consultant for cryptanalysis.

The codebreakers at Bletchley Park are credited with hastening Nazi defeat by two years, and saving thousands of lives.

Post-War Career

On 1945, Turing was awarded the Order of the British Empire for his wartime service, though the circumstances surrounding the award were not disclosed, as his contributions to the war effort were still classified.

In 1945 Alan began working at the National Physical Laboratory. There he wrote *Proposed Electronic Calculator* wherein he detailed the circuitry, hardware, coding, and even cost expectation for the Automatic Computing Engine.

The ACE was a continuation of Turing's 1936 concept of a stored program computer that gave rise to the idea of the Turing Machine. However, now that electronic advances had been made, and Turing himself was much more well versed in computing due to his experiences at Bletchley Park, the theoretical concept of a Turing Machine could, potentially, become a reality.

Machines at the time were essentially single use apparatuses. They were built to perform one function, and performing that function was the only thing they did. If you wanted a machine to perform a different function you would need to rewire it completely. Turing's computer would have programs installed into a it that could perform different functions based on the instructions in the program.

Interestingly, Alan didn't seem to care that much that his concept of the ACE would revolutionize machinery, and basically invent modern computer science. He was more interested in creating machines that mimic the functioning of a human brain. He said, "In working on the ACE I am more interested in the possibility of producing models of the action of the brain than in the practical applications to computing."

In 1946 Turing and his team at the National Physical Laboratory worked on a program library for the ACE, even before the computer itself was built. The Laboratory did not have the funding to begin to build the physical computer. One story says that the NPL didn't believe Alan's proposed budget was sufficient, and that they were unsure some of his plans would work out. However, because he had gotten his information from his work at Bletchley Park, Alan could not disclose to the Laboratory how he knew his plans and figures were sound, so the project was delayed.

Alan became increasingly frustrated with the delay in manufacturing the ACE and, in 1947, he returned to Cambridge for a sabbatical year, with the expectation that he would come back to work at the NPL when he had completed his year of independent research.

That is not what ended up happening. Manchester University scouted Turing for a position in their computing lab. In 1948 he was appointed the position of Reader in the Mathematics Department at Manchester's Victoria University. Turing resigned from the NPL, breaking the implied terms of his sabbatical, and greatly infuriating his former colleagues at the National Physical Laboratory.

Turing was to work on Manchester's own stored program computer, the Manchester Mark 1. In April of 1949 the Mark 1 was operational and, in the same year, Turing became Deputy Director of the Computing Lab at Manchester University.

Turing continued to be fascinated by the idea of a computer as a mechanical human mind that possesses all the capabilities of the working human brain. Of the Manchester Mark 1 he said, "This is only a foretaste of what is to come, and only the shadow of what is going to be. We have to have some experience with the machine before we really know its capabilities. It may take years before we settle down to the new possibilities, but I do not see why it should not enter any of the fields normally covered by the human intellect and eventually compete on equal terms."

In 1950 the Pilot ACE was built without Turing's aid at the National Physical Laboratory.

It ran its first program on May 10th, 1950 and was, for quite some time, the world's fastest computer. Though he was not present for the actual building of the machine, and his full vision of the ACE was not actually created until after his death, he is still credited as the genius behind the machine's invention.

In 1950 Alan wrote the paper *Computing Machinery and Intelligence*. It was an early foray into the concept of artificial intelligence, and a continuation of Alan's interest in building mechanical a "brain". In his paper he asked the question, "Are there imaginable digital computers which would do well in the *imitation game*?"

The Imitation Game was a party game where a man and a woman were separated from the rest of the guests, and from each other, and the crowd had to attempt to tell which person was which, based on their typewritten answers to several questions. However, each player was trying to convince the guessers that they were the other player.

Turing's test of artificial intelligence, aptly named the Turing Test, works in much the same way. The idea is that you have two humans, A and B, and one machine, that are all separated from each other. Human A must then ask Human B and the machine a series of typewritten questions. If Human A can't tell which answers are coming from Human B, and which are coming from the machine, the machine is said to have passed the test, and have some measure of intelligence.

The questions must be typewritten so as not to rely on the machine's grasp of spoken language. The results of the test also don't rely on the machine producing the correct answer to the question, just a coherent, human-like answer.

Building on this work computer scientists engineered a reverse Turing Test so that a computer may recognize when it is interacting with a human, rather than another computer. CAPTCHA, the skewed image of an alphanumeric code you have to type into a website before doing something like buying concert tickets or leaving a comment on a blog post, protects the website from spam or other misuse from automated systems.

In 1952 Alan set his sights on a different kind of science. Where he had been mostly involved in mathematics and computer science thus far in his adult life, he now became interested in chemistry as it related to animal biology. He specifically wanted to look at morphogenesis, the process by which animals develop spots and patterns on their skin, scaled, or fur, or how plants develop certain patterns on their leaves. Turing published a paper called *The Chemical Basis of Morphogenesis*.

In this paper Turing proposed a process called intercellular reaction-diffusion. Identical cells are either inhibited or excited by various chemicals moving through the system. The cells then either present a certain characteristic, or suppress it. This process produces a pattern like a zebra's stripes, or a leopard's spots. These ideas remained theoretical, as Alan was more a computer scientists than a biologist. However, his ideas are still being looked into today as the possible basis for certain patterns on animals.

Later Life and Convictions

In December of 1951 Alan met and began a relationship with a 19 year old man named Arnold Murray. Alan suspected Arnold of stealing money from him after they spent the night together at Alan's house. Arnold denied stealing from him, but did admit he was in some debt, prompting Alan to lend him money on several occasions.

On January 23rd 1952, Alan came home to find his house had been burgled. Nothing of much value had been taken, though a pocketwatch that was a family heirloom was missing. Regardless of the monetary value of what was stolen, the robbery was still a disturbing occurrence. In early February, Arnold admitted to Alan that his friend, Harry, was the one who robbed him.

Alan went to the police to report the identity of the robber to find that Harry had already been apprehended on unrelated charges. While reporting what he knew, Alan was questioned about his relationship with Murray. He admitted to police their relationship was of a sexual nature. Alan and Arnold were both arrested, and charged with "gross indecency" under Section 11 of the Criminal Law Amendment Act 1885.

This act, also known as the Labouchere Amendment, made homosexual acts, in cases where sodomy could not be proven, illegal. The act was replaced just 15 years later with the Sexual Offences Act 1967 which decriminalized homosexual acts between two consenting males, in private, so long as both individuals were aged 21 or older.

The initial committal proceedings were on February 27th, 1952. Turing's solicitor did not argue for his innocence as, under the laws of the time, Alan was technically guilty. His council and his family advised him to plead guilty. In the trial on March 31st, Alan pled guilty to the charges he faced. He was given the option between imprisonment, or probation and a hormone treatment. He chose the latter.

Arnold Murray was let off with a conditional discharge; essentially a probation period where he would not be charged for the crime at hand, on the condition that he was not arrested for any similar crimes in a stated period.

The hormone treatment consisted of a year of stilboestrol injections. This substance was a synthetic oestrogen that was meant to lower

Turing's sex drive. The end result was essentially a chemical castration. The injections rendered him sterile, and allegedly caused a condition known as gynaecomastia, an increase in the glandular tissue around the nipples due to a hormone imbalance, giving the appearance of female breasts.

Alan also had his security clearances removed because of the conviction. As a result, he was no longer able to work on his cryptographic consultancy for the Government Communications Headquarters.

Death Theories

On June 8th, 1954 Alan Turing's housekeeper found him dead in his bedroom. A half-eaten apple lay by his bedside. A subsequent inquest determined the cause of his death was suicide by cyanide poisoning. Turing had allegedly laced the apple with the chemical, and ate it before bed. He, like his father, was cremated at Woking Crematorium, and his ashes were scattered on the grounds.

Several Turing biographers (including the director of the hit film *The Imitation Game*, based on Turing's life) believe his death was, in fact, a suicide, based on Alan's obsession with *Snow White and the Seven Dwarfs*. Turing was apparently enchanted by the film, and particularly interested in the scene where the Evil Queen dips the apple into poison before feeding it to Snow White. They believe his suicide was a reenactment of this scene.

This scenario feeds into the narrative that has grown up around Turing since his death. He has been painted as an oppressed, hounded individual who became so depressed by his conviction and subsequent punishment that he took his own life. However, many do not believe this version of Turing existed in reality.

Jack Copeland, a professor of Philosophy at the University of Canterbury, and an expert on Turing's life, has laid out many pieces of evidence pointing to Turing's death being an accident.

Copeland claims it wasn't unusual for Alan to take an apple to bed, and that he often didn't finish it. The mere existence of the half-eaten fruit on the scene is far from definitive proof of a suicide. There is also the fairly ridiculous fact that the apple was never even tested for cyanide. The idea that Alan killed himself with a poison-laced apple was just an assumption made by investigators. The apple could have accidentally come into contact with the substance, or could have been completely free of cyanide altogether.

Deniers of the suicide theory also point out the fact that, not only did Alan not leave a suicide note of any kind, he actually had reminders on his desk of what needed to be completed in the following week, a list that would obviously be unnecessary if Alan was planning on taking his life.

Then there is the odd timing of his death. Those who think he committed suicide say he was so depressed by his conviction and punishment that he became suicidal. However, Alan went through an entire year of hormone therapy, and, at the time of his death, yet another year had passed since the therapy had ended. He was two years removed from the worst of the scandal, and his punishment was over.

In that two years he was said to have borne his punishment with "amused fortitude". Friends and family said he showed no signs that he was particularly distressed by the sentencing. Copeland has said, "In a way, we have, in modern times been recreating the narrative of Turing's life, and we have recreated him as an unhappy young man who committed suicide. But the evidence is not there".

Indeed, friends say he was in his usual high spirits the week before his death, throwing a tea party for his young neighbour, and staying the weekend at his close friend Robin

Gandy's house. Gandy said he, "seemed, if anything, happier than usual."

It is not unusual for those who have decided on suicide to suddenly brighten before their death; feeling a weight lifted from their shoulders, as they know their suffering will soon be over. However, this doesn't necessarily seem to be the case with Turing. It seems he never experienced the sadness or despondency that usually precedes that sudden upswing. By all accounts, Alan was as upbeat as ever before his death.

That being said, Alan was always an eccentric personality with fairly odd mannerisms. A friend, Geoffrey Jefferson, described Alan's behavior as, "so unversed in worldly ways, so childlike, so non-conformist, so very absent-minded... a sort of scientific Shelley." He always seemed slightly disconnected from reality.

Alan was said to lock his tea mug to the radiator when he was finished work for the day; he would wear a gas mask to work when his allergies were acting up; he sometimes wore a necktie to keep his trousers up, instead of an actual belt; and apparently more than once he would show up to work in his pajamas. A colleague even said Alan once came to work with an alarm clock tied around his waist. He was generally disheveled and always quite absent-minded about his appearance and how he came across to others.

Some close to Alan seemed to notice that the stress of the war and his important work had somewhat gotten to him. Though he was always eccentric, he seemed somewhat manic nearing the end of the war.

There was a story circulating that Alan had withdrawn all his money from his bank accounts and buried the cash on the grounds at Bletchley so he would have access to his money in the event of a German invasion. This story paints the picture of a paranoid, distressed individual who was unnecessarily worried about the future.

His brother, John, however, saw nothing particularly odd about Alan's behavior. Of the story of Alan burying all his money, John said, "In fact, he did nothing of the kind. He had decided that if there were a German invasion, banking accounts would be useless, so he bought some silver ingots for use on the black market. These he trundled in an ancient perambulator and buried in a field (not at Bletchley), where he made a sketch map of their position so he could find them after the war. After the war, he enlisted the help of his friend, Donald Michie, to dig up these ingots - using, typically, a homemade metal detector - but the heavy ingots were by now well on their way to Australia and were never seen again."

John saw this as Alan taking some precautions against a possible German invasion; securing his future. That is not to say that John believed his brother was at all in his right mind, or that his death was an accident. John did believe Alan had committed suicide, though, mostly at his mother's urging, he attempted to find any evidence that it was an accident.

Whether or not Alan became unhinged after the war is difficult to prove. Some saw him in high spirits and never saw him any other way; some thought his behavior was even odder than usual; and some just thought Alan was being authentically Alan. There is no way to know for certain at this point whether or not he was acting particularly unusually, or what his state of mind really was.

Upon investigation of Alan's body, the coroner said, "I am forced to the conclusion that this was a deliberate act. In a man of his type, one never knows what his mental processes are going to do next." He claimed that "the balance of [Turing's] mind was disturbed" at the time of his death, which led him to suicide. It seems the coroner was aware of Alan's trademark eccentricities. However, it is unscientific to assume Alan's death was a suicide just because he occasionally acted oddly and could potentially have wanted to kill himself. Ultimately there is no way the coroner could have known Alan's particular mental state at the time of his death, leading many to question the man's conclusions.

Andrew Hodges, Turing's biographer sums up the confusion around Alan's death beautifully in his book *Alan Turing: The Enigma.* Hodges writes, "Alan Turing's death came as a shock to those who knew him. It fell into no clear sequence of events. Nothing was explicit - there was no warning, no note of explanation. It seemed an isolated act of self-annihilation...There was no simple connection in the minds of those who had seen him in the previous two years. On the contrary, his reaction had been so different from the wilting, disgraced, fearful, hopeless figure expected by fiction and drama, that those who had seen it could hardly believe that he was dead."

A study of Alan's physical state at the time of his death does not necessarily make the picture any clearer. Looking at the autopsy report, Copeland notes that the distribution of cyanide in Turing's organs was more consistent with inhalation than with ingestion. This would make sense, as Alan had a fairly small, poorly-ventilated laboratory in his house. At the time of his death he was working on electroplating spoons with gold, a process which requires potassium cyanide. Turing could easily have inhaled cyanide fumes and been slowly poisoned to death in his sleep that night.

Alan's marked disinterest in safety procedures also points to an accidental poisoning. Turing seemed to be the very picture of a mad scientist. He had hooked wires from his electrolysis experiments up to the light fixtures of his house and had apparently been so careless with electricity in the past that he had given himself severe electric shocks. He also tended to taste chemicals to figure out what they were.

Though an extremely intellectual person, Alan was known all his life for his absent-mindedness. His mother believed for the rest of her life that her son's death was an accident borne from his characteristic carelessness. Some believe that it was, indeed, cyanide inhalation that caused his death, but that Alan poisoned himself on purpose and made it look accidental in order to protect his mother from the idea that he would take his own life.

This last theory does not line up with what was revealed after his death about Alan's feelings toward his mother. John Turing visited Alan's psychiatrist, Franz Greenbaum, to attempt to glean from him what his brother's mental state was leading up to his death. The psychiatrist gave John two journals of Alan's wherein he had written pages and pages of notes on how he hated his mother. John kept this information from their mother. She never knew of her son's feelings about her, and continued to search for evidence of an accidental poisoning. In light of this information it is rather unlikely that Alan staged a suicide to look like an accident in order to protect his mother, or anyone else for that matter.

One thing that could possibly point to his death as a suicide is the fact that Alan re-wrote his will a short time before he died. On February 11th, 1954 he updated his will, making his friend Nick Furbank the executor. Alan left money to his brother's family, his housekeeper, three friends, and his mother. John believed the money that went to his mother was more out of a sense of familial duty, rather than because he actually wanted to give her money.

It is not necessarily unusual for such a young man to have a will though, as many people expect to outlive their parents, it could be considered strange that Alan included his mother in it at all. This could be evidence that Alan considered suicide. However, the will also specified that Alan's housekeeper was to get an additional £10 for each year she had worked for him after the end of 1953. This provision obviously makes no sense if Alan was actually planning to end his life soon after writing the will.

Another theory about Turing's death is much more sinister. Author Roger Bristow claims Alan was murdered by the FBI, who then made it look like a suicide. Bristow says that Turing was working on secret cryptanalysis projects for the Americans before his death. Dubbed Operation Verona, the project was allegedly centered on deciphering radio signals to locate Russian agents undercover in America. Bristow alleges that Turing must have found out sensitive secrets that would embarrass or otherwise harm the government.

The author points out that there is a note on the post mortem report by the pathologist who examined Turing that read, "Death appears to be due to violence." He seems to think that the final verdict on Turing's death is that it was caused by extreme bodily harm, and that the cyanide found in his body was either administered to him during the murder, or was incidental; a side-effect of Turing's careless lab practices. Bristow said, "I don't know if someone who has taken cyanide is able to beat themselves up, but it seems totally incompatible with the line used previously."

There are others who speculate that Alan was murdered simply because he knew too much about cryptanalysis, and the British government's code cracking procedures. He did have high level knowledge of government secrets, and he had lost his security clearance as he was technically a convicted criminal. Some think this put him in a vulnerable position and he was taken out before he could leak government secrets, or be made by enemies to reveal them.

It has also been suggested that he was murdered because his homosexuality somehow put him at risk for blackmail schemes. However, it is well documented that Alan did not hide is orientation, and he had already been convicted of gross indecency, so there was not really much of a threat to him.

The fact that the apple was never tested for cyanide, but the inquest claimed that it was the cause of his death is evidence of either gross incompetence in the police department, or of some sort of cover up. In 2013, human rights activist Peter Tatchell wrote to the British Prime Minister asking for a new inquest into Alan Turing's death. Though he admits there is "no evidence that Turing was murdered by state agents", he does point out that "the fact that this possibility has never been investigated is a major failing."

However he died, the inquest into Alan Turing's death was nowhere near as thorough as it should have been. There are far too many completely plausible and totally uninvestigated possibilities as to how he may have died to ever know for sure whether it was suicide, an accident, or murder.

It is obvious, though, that Alan was treated harshly and unfairly by many throughout his life for both his strange eccentricities, and his open homosexuality. Though he seemed to many to be unfazed by his persecution, his brother firmly believed it was the treatment Alan received from others that led him to take his own life. John Turing said of his brother, "He was a complex man and much loved by many. Had he been better understood when he was young - and if I, among others, had treated him with more consideration - he might be alive today."

Pardoning

In August of 2009, programmer and Oxford alum John Graham-Cumming started a petition that urged the British government to apologize for prosecuting Turing as gay. It received over 30,000 signatures and got the attention of government officials.

In a statement on September 10th 2009, British Prime Minister Gordon Brown said, "Thousands of people have come together to demand justice for Alan Turing and recognition of the appalling way he was treated. While Turing was dealt with under the law of the time and we can't put the clock back, his treatment was of course utterly unfair and I am pleased to have the chance to say how deeply sorry I and we all are for what happened to him ... So on behalf of the British government, and all those who live freely thanks to Alan's work I am very proud to say: we're sorry, you deserved so much better."

An apology, however, is not the same as a pardon. It acknowledges a misdoing, but does not fix it. Turing's conviction was still technically on the books and he was still a criminal in the eyes of the law.

John Leech, the Member of Parliament for Manchester-Withington submitted several bills to parliament that would overturn Turing's conviction. He claimed that, due to Alan's position as a British hero who helped win the war, and current society's completely different view on homosexuality, it was "ultimately just embarrassing" that his conviction still stood.

An e-petition for a full pardoning of Alan Turing, circulated by William Jones in 2011, garnered over 37,000 signatures. Jones and Leech campaigned together to bring attention to their mission. They met opposition from some law officials, including Lord McNally who claimed that, though Turing's persecution was "both cruel and absurd", he was technically rightfully convicted under the laws of the time.

Homosexual sexual acts were illegal, and Turing did plead guilty to the charges. There have been many laws in history that have been overturned, but that does not mean that certain acts were never illegal, or that the government should undertake the daunting and ultimately fruitless task of posthumously pardoning everyone who ever did something illegal that is no longer illegal.

Some felt that pardoning just one person because of his celebrity would be unfair to the many ordinary men who were also cruelly persecuted under the same laws. Others believed the pardoning of Alan Turing would either be a symbolic pardoning of all other men affected, or be the first step in actually officially pardoning all the others.

On July 26th, 2012 a bill was introduced in the House of Lords for a pardon of Turing under Section 11 of the Criminal Law Amendment Act. The bill had massive support from the scientific community. Stephen Hawking wrote in *The Daily Telegraph* an open letter to Prime Minister David Cameron urging him to act on the pardon.

The bill passed on its third reading in October 2012, and on December 24th, 2013 Queen Elizabeth II signed the official pardon of Alan Turing.

As it turned out Turing's pardon was the first step in the efforts to pardon others who were likewise convicted. In September 2016 a law, nicknamed the Alan Turing Law, was proposed that would retroactively pardon men convicted under indecency laws for acts related to homosexuality in England and Wales. The law that came into effect in 2017, posthumously pardoned 50,000 men, including Oscar Wilde, and gives the option for 15,000 still-living men to apply for an official pardon.

Conclusion

Hugh Alexander, Alan's colleague at Bletchley Park said of Alan, "There should be no question in anyone's mind that Turing's work was the biggest factor in Hut 8's success. In the early days, he was the only cryptographer who thought the problem worth tackling and not only was he primarily responsible for the main theoretical work within the Hut, but he also shared with Welchman and Keen the chief credit for the invention of the bombe.

It is always difficult to say that anyone is 'absolutely indispensable', but if anyone was indispensable to Hut 8, it was Turing. The pioneer's work always tends to be forgotten when experience and routine later make everything seem easy and many of us in Hut 8 felt that the magnitude of Turing's contribution was never fully realised by the outside world."

Alexander did not know how true that sentiment would end up being. Today we take so many things for granted that were originally completely revolutionary ideas conceived by Alan Turing.

Many say that World War Two would have been won by the Allies eventually, with or without the intelligence gleaned by Turing and his team, but that it was won much faster thanks to the codebreaking at Bletchley Park. However, it is impossible to know whether that really is the case.

The breaking of naval Enigma messages ensured the safety of Allied supply lines in the Atlantic, which brought food, weapons, and other much needed supplies to Allied soldiers. That corridor was also essential for ferrying troops from America to Europe for the D-Day invasions. The war truly may not have gone the same way had Turing not conceived of the Bombe, and broken the naval Enigma.

Without Turing we may not even have the computer as we know it today. Turing was one of the first to conceive of a stored-memory computer that would allow a machine to perform more than one function simply by inputting different programs into it. This is the basis of the computer we all use today, the concept of which has been translated into smartphones, which can perform countless functions in seconds from wherever you happen to be.

Hugh Alexander died in 1974, unaware of the recognition Turing would eventually receive for his genius, and his many contributions to mathematics, computer science, the war effort, and even biology.

Many plaques and statues have been placed at significant places in Turing's life in recognition of his accomplishments, and as apologies for how he was treated. The plaque on one such statue reads, "Father of computer science, mathematician, logician, wartime codebreaker, victim of prejudice".

Turing was named as one of Time Magazine's 100 Most Important People of the 20th Century, and is on BBC's list of the Top 100 Greatest Britons. He has many educational halls, buildings, and laboratories at various universities named after him.

Many people have also immortalized Alan Turing in books and movies; notably, Benedict Cumberbatch in the Oscar winning film *The Imitation Game* based on Andrew Hodges' in-depth biography *Alan Turing: The Enigma*.

He could even be said to be a pioneer of gay rights. Though he did not actively campaign for any freedoms for homosexual men, Alan did not hide his orientation, even in a time when homosexuality was illegal. He lived freely as a gay man for most of his life, admitting his sexual preference even to his potential wife, Joan Clarke. He was also the impetus for the retroactive pardoning of thousands of gay men who were convicted under indecency laws at the time.

While some of his colleagues and admirers believed he died not getting the recognition he deserved, Alan Turing is now becoming known as one of the most influential humans of the 20th century. It is not often you can definitively state that the world would be a drastically different place without a certain individual, but with Alan Turing that is exactly the case.

Printed in Great Britain
by Amazon